A TALKING POINTS BOOK BY
VAUGHAN ROBERTS

ASSISTED SUICIDE

thegoodbook
COMPANY

Assisted Suicide
© Vaughan Roberts/The Good Book Company, 2017

Published by
The Good Book Company
Tel (UK): 0333 123 0880
Tel (North America): (1) 866 244 2165
International: +44 (0) 208 942 0880
Email (UK): info@thegoodbook.co.uk
Email (North America): info@thegoodbook.com

Websites
North America: www.thegoodbook.com
UK & Europe: www.thegoodbook.co.uk
Australia: www.thegoodbook.com.au
New Zealand: www.thegoodbook.co.nz

Unless otherwise indicated, Scripture quotations are from
The Holy Bible, New International Version, NIV Copyright © 1973,
1978, 1984, 2011 by Biblica, Inc.

ISBN: 9781784981938 | Printed in Denmark

Design by André Parker

CONTENTS

INTRODUCTION
TALKING POINTS

The world is changing. Fast.

And not just politics, technology and communication, but our whole culture, morality and attitudes. Christians living in Western culture have enjoyed the benefit of being in a world which largely shared our assumptions about what is fundamentally right and wrong. We can no longer assume that this is the case.

In two short generations we have moved to a widespread adoption of liberal values, many of which are in conflict with the teaching of the Bible. Increasingly, believers are finding themselves to be the misunderstood minority, and feeling at odds with where the world seems to be heading.

Let's not deny it: some of this has been good. Christians have often failed to discern the difference between our own cultural values, and those that are demanded by Scripture. We are as prone to bigotry as others. We have much to repent of in our attitudes towards the freedom and role of women in society, and in our lack of compassion and understanding towards, for example, those who have wrestled with same-sex attraction.

But now again, we find ourselves in unfamiliar territory and ill-equipped to deal with it. Sometimes it's easier to protest and rage against the tide of history than to go back to our Bibles and think carefully about what God is saying—holding up society's views, and our own, to the truth-revealing mirror that is God's word.

At our best, we Christians have been in the forefront of social reform. Think of the great nineteenth-century reformers of the slave trade, prisons and poverty: William Wilberforce, Elizabeth Fry and Lord Shaftesbury. But now we find ourselves on the back foot, unable to articulate a clear response to a pressing question of our day. And even when we have understood God's mind on a particular issue, we have struggled to apply it compassionately in our speech and in our relationships.

This short series of books is an attempt to help ordinary Christians start to think constructively about a range of issues—moral, ethical and cultural—that run against the grain for those who name Christ as Lord. They are an attempt to stimulate believers to start talking with each other as we search the Scriptures together. Their aim is to help us think biblically, constructively and compassionately, and not to feel intimidated when we are challenged or questioned, or, perhaps worse, remain silent.

WHAT THIS BOOK IS NOT...

In such a short book, we cannot hope to answer all the questions you may have about how to think about ageing, illness and assisted suicide. Nor can we address the many practical challenges you may be facing with family or friends, or personally.

Nor does this book present a thorough treatment of all the Bible has to say on these questions. If that is what you are hungry for, there will be other, longer, and perhaps more technical books that will help you dig deeper.

WHAT THIS BOOK IS...

Rather, our aim is to give you an accessible introduction to the many questions that surround the issue of assisted suicide, and a starting point for constructive discussion between Christian believers and with others. It aims to give you a cultural briefing on where we are with this question, and some pointers on how Christians should think, talk and act.

But we also hope that it takes us all beyond the issue—to a genuine compassion and love for those who are caught up in some way with these questions. They may be questions that are deeply personal to you. They may be questions that are thrown at you in a proud, assertive and hostile way. Or they may be questions that are real because they affect a close family member or friend. Whatever your situation, we hope this book will be a first step towards understanding the landscape, and an encouragement to know and share the love and hope we have in Christ.

Tim Thornborough
Series Editor
January 2017

euthanasia

[yoo-th*uh*-**ney**-zee-uh]

noun: **euthanasia**

1. the painless killing of a patient suffering
   from an incurable and painful disease or in
   an irreversible coma.

synonyms:

   mercy killing, assisted suicide, physician-assisted
   suicide; merciful release, happy release;
   rare quietus

[Source: dictionary.com]

*"I will give no deadly medicine to any one if asked,
nor suggest any such counsel."*
The Hippocratic Oath

"My Life. My death. My choice"
Assisted Dying slogan

*"Those who have a terminal illness and are in
great pain should have the right to choose to end
their lives, and those who help them should be free
from prosecution."*
Stephen Hawking, physicist

*"Euthanasia kills the patient twice—once when we say,
'Yes, your life is not worth living,' and then when we
help him die."*
Dr Peter Saunders, physician and medical ethicist

*"This is not a matter of life versus death, but about the
timing and manner of an inevitable death."*
Dr. Marcia Angell, Harvard Medical School

"Thou shalt not kill."
The sixth commandment, Exodus 20 v 13 (KJV)

*"All flesh is grass,
and all its beauty is like the flower of the field.
The grass withers, the flower fades…
… but the word of our God will stand forever."*
Isaiah 40 v 6-8

A COMPLEX PROBLEM

CHAPTER ONE

The focus of this little book is the complex subject of assisted suicide. It is complex because it needs to be thought about deeply on philosophical, medical, biblical, legal and ethical levels. But it would be a mistake to leave it there, because it is also a deeply personal issue.

In 2008, **Frances Inglis**, injected her son Tom with a massive overdose of heroin, which ended his life. Tom had become brain-damaged, after an accident; he was paralysed, doubly incontinent and unable to communicate. Francis, a mother of three who worked with adults and children with learning and physical disabilities, considered what she did a "mercy killing". In court, she admitted killing him, saying, "I did it with love in my heart"—as his mother, she couldn't bear to see him in that state. Under the law she was convicted of murder and given a life sentence. Frances was released after serving five years in prison.

Around the same time, **Kay Gilderdale** was also in court. Her 31-year-old daughter Lynn had been paralysed since suffering with chronic fatigue syndrome (CFS) from the age of 14. In frequent agony, she received a constant supply of the pain-killer morphine through a syringe driver into her veins. Unlike Tom Inglis in the previous story, Lynn was able to communicate through sign language, and participated in online forums through a hand-held computer. She laid bare her frustrations, describing her "miserable excuse for a life" and adding, "I can't keep hanging on to an ever-diminishing hope that I might one day be well again".

One night she pleaded with her mother for over an hour to end her life. Kay surrendered to her wishes and gave her daughter two large doses of morphine, which Lynn self-administered. But the dose did not prove fatal, and so Kay injected her with more morphine, and injected three syringes of air into her veins. Lynn eventually died of morphine poisoning. After a jury found Kay not guilty of attempted murder, she was convicted of the lesser charge of aiding and abetting suicide. The sentence was suspended, so she walked free from court.

Kate Cheney, 85, had terminal cancer and told her doctor that she wanted assisted suicide, which is legal in her home state of Oregon, USA. The doctor was concerned that she didn't meet the required criteria for mental competence because of dementia, so he declined to write the requested prescription and instead referred her to a psychiatrist, as required by law. She was accompanied to the psychiatric consultation by her daughter. The psychiatrist found that Kate had a loss of short-term memory, and reported that it appeared that her daughter had more interest in Cheney's assisted suicide than did the patient herself. He wrote in his report that while the assisted suicide seemed consistent with Kate's values, "she does not seem to be explicitly pushing for this". He also determined that Kate did not have the "very high capacity required to weigh options about assisted suicide", and therefore declined to authorize the lethal prescription.

Reports suggest that Kate seemed to accept the psychiatrist's verdict, but that her daughter did not. Her daughter viewed the guidelines protecting her mother's life as obstacles, and in a press interview she called them a "roadblock" to Kate's right to die, and demanded a second opinion. This was provided by a clinical psychologist, who expressed concern about familial pressure, writing that Kate's decision to die "may be influenced by her family's wishes". Despite these reservations, the psychologist determined that Kate was competent to choose death. She was given pills, which she later took to end her own life. This case is one of many that has given concern—in places where assisted suicide is legal—that the process is open to abuse. It may be possible to circumvent safeguards by "shopping" for an agreeable professional, and there is a real danger of family pressure.[1]

Stories such as these appear regularly in the media in the context of the ongoing discussions about whether assisted suicide should be made legal. They illustrate the complexity of the subject and the potential dangers associated with the relaxation of the law. But, above all, they remind us that behind the moral and legal debates are real people facing extremely difficult circumstances. It may be that you know that all too well from your own experience, perhaps because you, or someone you love, suffers from a terrible progressive condition, such as Alzheimer's, or has received a terminal diagnosis.

As I was preparing to write this book, my own father was told that he had terminal brain cancer, and he died a few months later. That has meant that I have not only been thinking about some of the issues raised in this book, but have also been

---

1 Find a fuller version and more stories at http://wrtl.org/assisted-suicide/personal-stories-assisted-suicide/ accessed January 2017.

very much living them as I have been writing. The whole experience has strengthened my conviction that assisted suicide should be firmly resisted, but it has also given me a more personal insight into the intense pain involved in the circumstances that often trigger the discussion.

Many people live with a desire to end their lives. Perhaps you or someone close to you is one of them, whether because of illness, mental distress, a concern not to be a burden to others or fear that a progressive condition will make life unbearable. We all know in principle that we are mortal and that death is inevitable, but there are times when those realities especially press upon us. What the apostle Peter says in his letter resonates with us all:

All people are like grass, and all their glory is like the flower of the field. The grass withers, and the flower falls…"   1 Peter 1 v 24

The question is: should others be free to help us end our lives? How can we navigate this complex area filled with heart-wrenching stories and painful choices? Peter points us towards the source of the help we need in the words that finish his sentence:

… but the word of the Lord endures for ever.

SOME DEFINITIONS

The words we use as we talk about this subject are important. Those who argue that assisted suicide should be legal often use euphemisms such as "merciful release" or "easeful death", and many now prefer to use the term "assisted dying". The British organisation which used to be called the Voluntary Euthanasia Society has changed its name to Dignity in Dying. The effect of such language is to soften the reality and imply that what is being proposed is only designed to ensure good care as someone's life comes to an end, rather than being an active intervention to end their life. So it is important that we understand the meaning of the relevant terms.

Suicide. The voluntary and intentional act of taking one's own life.

Assisted suicide. Helping someone else to end their life. Under the Suicide Act 1961 it is illegal in England and Wales to "aid, abet, counsel or procure the suicide of another or an attempt of another to commit suicide".

Euthanasia. The killing of another person with the intention of relieving their suffering.

Voluntary euthanasia. The killing of someone who has asked for their life to be ended.

Involuntary euthanasia. Death occurs as a result of a decision by someone other than the person killed. This may be because the individual is unable to give consent because of their mental or physical condition.

Physician-assisted suicide. Assistance provided by a doctor in the suicide of a patient who has chosen to end their life.

Palliative medicine/care. A branch of healthcare that specialises in the relief of the pain and distress caused by an incurable illness. The main goal is to help people live as well as possible during the time they have left, rather than seeking to cure them.

Hospice. A hospital or care home that specialises in treating and caring for those who are dying from a terminal disease.

A GROWING PROBLEM
CHAPTER TWO

The poet W. H. Auden wrote that death is behind everything, "like the distant roll of thunder at a picnic."[2] We're aware of its impending approach, threatening to spoil everything, but we'd rather not think about it. Despite their inevitability, death and dying are not subjects for polite conversation or everyday discussion.

INSTITUTIONALISED DEATH

Perhaps part of the problem is that we have *institutionalised* death and those who are dying. Wind back the clock 50 years and the majority of people would have died in their own homes, being cared for by their families. Today, most people die in hospital,

---

2   Quoted in *Marginalia* by Tom Chivers (London: Penned in the Margins, 2014)

a care home or a hospice, cared for by professional staff, and less than 20% die at home. This change has had the general effect of *removing* death from the everyday experience of families and communities. It is hidden, so that many adults have never seen a dead body.

In addition, the wonderful advances in medical understanding over the last 50 years have greatly extended the life expectancy we have. In 1960 the average age of death was around 70 in the UK and North America. Now we can have a reasonable level of confidence that we will live another 10 years on top of that.

Doctors report that many patients, even those who are in their 70s and 80s, are shocked when they are given a terminal diagnosis—as though they never conceived that death was a possibility. Such is our disconnection from the reality and inevitability of death.

AGEING POPULATION

Ten more years of life may sound attractive, but they bring with them a reduced expectation of the quality of life. Dementia and disability become more likely the older we get, and the cost of treating such conditions can be enormous, as many older people are forced to move into care or nursing homes. The average age of the population in most countries in the Western world is rising dramatically, as are the costs of social welfare.

As I write this, the news is filled with dire warnings of the care system collapsing under the load, while politicians appear to dither and scratch their heads about how the enormous cost of caring for the elderly and infirm will be met.

In addition, there is the fragmenting of family and community life. In years past, families were larger, and often lived in close proximity to each other: in the same town, village or city suburb. Their lives were more deeply interconnected, and matters of care were more easily dealt with through these natural networks.

Now we have smaller families, and greater mobility. That places a greater burden on only a few family members, who are likely to live further away from each other, thus reducing their ability to offer practical help, and to weave caring for others into their everyday lives.

These are not inconsequential problems. Caring for elderly parents and relatives is a major feature of life for many people. Some give up productive work, earnings and careers so they can look after ailing elderly family members. For others the solution will be to sell a family home, and spend whatever savings are available to pay for professional care, perhaps leaving little to pass on to the next generation. In countries with strong state-backed medical and social-care provision, like the UK, there is a safety net. But in other parts of the world, those who are elderly, infirm or with dementia, and who have no local family to help, can often slide into poverty and isolation.

They may have 10 extra years of life, but for many the prospect is miserable. It is easy to understand why, in these conditions, support for the legalisation of assisted suicide has grown. Surely, it is argued, this will both benefit those individuals who wish to take that option, by ending their suffering, and also help society, by avoiding a great deal of exhausting and expensive care. But, as I will argue in chapter 4, all such thoughts should be firmly resisted.

A LONG-STANDING PROHIBITION

It is not just the elderly for whom assisted suicide is an issue. Many others, like those in the stories in the last chapter, prefer to choose death when the prospect is a life with pain, or disability, or if they find being cared for humiliating.

Although the advances in medical treatment have been spectacular, there is, as yet, no known cure for many debilitating conditions. And there is no road back to full health for many who suffer accidents.

Given the choice between a quick ending and a life of pain, it is not surprising that some will search for ways to bring their lives to a swift end. These pressures have always existed, but for many centuries it has been illegal to help someone commit suicide. The foundations of this prohibition are found in the Bible and in ancient medical tradition.

The sixth commandment in the Bible states,"You shall not murder" (Exodus 20 v 6). Behind these words lie a general principle, repeated throughout scripture, that God is both the *author* and *giver* of life. Our lives belong to him. He breathed life into our bodies and only he has the right to take life away.

> *"See now that I myself am he! There is no god besides me. I put to death and I bring to life, I have wounded and I will heal…"*
>
> Deuteronomy 32 v 39

A deep concern to avoid the taking of life is also found in classical medicine. In the 4th century BC the ancient Greek physician Hippocrates, considered the father of modern medicine, developed his famous "Hippocratic Oath" for doctors, which includes these words:

I will give no deadly medicine to anyone if asked, nor suggest any such counsel.

Doctors no longer take this oath, which also contains a promise not to perform abortions, but it has formed the backdrop to the ethical rules that doctors operate under: they are about healing and restoring life, not ending it.[3]

In countries informed by the Christian worldview, the prohibition of both suicide and assisted suicide stayed firmly in place for centuries. Understanding has grown over the years about the diminished responsibility that comes with mental illness, but even when suicide was decriminalised, the ban on assisted suicide remained firm.

THE MOVEMENT FOR CHANGE

Throughout the 20th century there was a growing movement for a change in the law. The debate led to the legalisation of assisted suicide, or voluntary euthanasia, in Colombia (1977), the Netherlands and Belgium (2002), and Canada in 2016. It was legal briefly in parts of Australia, before a state law was overturned. In the United States there are

---

3   This does not mean that doctors should always aim to prolong life at any cost. When death is approaching, their focus should be on relieving suffering. See page 59 for more on this.

assisted-dying laws restricted to terminally ill and mentally competent adults in Oregon, Montana, Washington, Vermont, California and Colorado.

Some of the consequences have been disturbing. The official 2013 report on the operation of the legislation in Washington stated that 61% of those who chose assisted suicide stated as one of the reasons for their decision their feeling that they were a burden on family, friends and caregivers.[4] In the Netherlands the number of people who have ended their lives due to "insufferable" mental illness has risen from 2 people in 2010 to 56 people in 2015.[5] And in Belgium the number of reported cases of assisted suicide has risen 89% in four years, from 953 in 2010 to 1,807 in 2013. The latter figure represents 1.7% of all deaths in Belgium.[6]

Euthanasia remains illegal in the UK, which is why almost 300 Britons have travelled to the Dignitas offices in Switzerland since 2002. The pressure to change the law to allow assisted suicide continues through pressure groups like Dignity in Dying.

---

4   Washington State Department of Health 2013 Death with Dignity Act Report, 7

5   http://www.telegraph.co.uk/news/2016/05/11/netherlands-sees-sharp-increase-in-people-choosing-euthanasia-du/

6   http://www.ieb-eib.org/fr/document/belgian-euthanasia-increases-by-89-in-four-years-382.html

It is against this backdrop of growing needs, pressures and opportunities that we turn to the arguments for and against euthanasia and assisted suicide.

THE RIGHT TO DIE?

CHAPTER THREE

A number of different arguments are made in support of assisted suicide.

1. PAIN

Most of the early arguments in favour of euthanasia focused on the issue of pain. If we see an animal in great distress, suffering an agonising death, we recognise that the humane thing to do is to put it out of its misery. Surely, it is argued, compassion demands that we allow the same approach for humans who want to hasten their death.

The fear of a painful end to life remains widespread, but advances in effective pain control and palliative care now mean that no one need die in agony. As a result, most advocates of assisted suicide focus on other factors.

2. FREEDOM

Whose Life is it Anyway? by British playwright Brian Clark was a TV drama that became a successful theatre production on Broadway in the 1970s. Set in a hospital room, the action revolves around Ken Harrison, a sculptor, who is paralysed from the neck down after a car accident and is determined to be allowed to die. Clark presents arguments both for and against euthanasia, and raises the question of the extent to which government should be allowed to interfere in the life of a private citizen. Ken is portrayed as a witty, intelligent man with a useless body, and he leaves the audience with conflicting feelings about his desire to end his life. He expresses the argument well when he says:

> *I do not wish to live at any price. Of course I would like to live, but as far as I am concerned I am dead already. I merely require the doctors to recognise the fact. I cannot accept this condition constitutes life in any real sense at all.*

For Ken, as for many in his situation, an illness or an accident that leads to an absence of freedom and choice makes them think that death is preferable, and so they believe they should have the right to be assisted in ending their lives. After all, "whose life is it anyway?" For many, the answer is obvious: "It's my life; it's mine to do with as I wish and to end as I choose".

In the words of the English philosopher John Stuart Mill:

Over himself, over his own body and mind, the individual is sovereign.

"I'm free! Free to live as I like. And free to die as I want. It is my body to do with as I wish." That fundamental conviction is the basis on which many people feel confident to say, "My life. My death. My choice."

This is the principle that underlies the other arguments advanced in favour of assisted suicide.

3. QUALITY OF LIFE

People who have had an active lifestyle find it difficult to conceive of enjoying life with diminished capacity for physical activity. Many more fear the onset of dementia, which will rob them of their abilities, interests and capacity to appreciate many of the pleasures of life.

What becomes clear from this argument is that much of the debate is driven not just by compassion for another person, but also by fear of what I myself might have to endure. It is a forward-looking argument that is fuelled by worry now. "I would hate to be in a nursing home like that." "I cannot conceive of life without reading, or walking the dog, or enjoying a pint at the pub." This is a very real fear, as we now have a 1 in 3 chance of developing dementia if we live beyond 70.

4. DEPENDENCE AND DIGNITY

The atheist philosopher Nietzsche said:

> *I want to die proudly when it is no longer possible to live properly.*

What he feared was the loss of dignity that comes with failing health and the consequent need to rely on others for the most simple of tasks: washing, getting dressed, eating. For many people the indignity of losing control of their bladder and bowels and having to wear a nappy (diaper) is embarrassing and unthinkable. In fact, according to surveys in countries where it is permitted, loss of dignity is now the most significant factor that propels people towards assisted suicide. But note again, it is an argument that is often driven by fear of the future, rather than something that is necessarily experienced in the present.

Sir Terry Pratchett, the British author of the *Discworld* novels, made a ground-breaking TV documentary on assisted death. Pratchett, who was suffering himself from early-onset Alzheimer's disease, followed Peter Smedley, a 71-year-old man suffering from motor-neurone disease (MND, also known as ALS), as he went to the Dignitas clinic in Switzerland. Mr Smedley chose to end his life prematurely before his condition worsened—as it progressed, the illness would have prevented him from swallowing and breathing, and he didn't want to get to that stage. In the final scene of the film, Mr Smedley takes a lethal dose of a barbiturate and dies with his wife, Sir Terry and two Dignitas staff alongside him.

The BBC executive who had commissioned the programme said at the time of its broadcast:

> *I hope this film transcends the arguments over legislation, policy and morality. It is an invitation to viewers to leave the debate behind and engage empathetically with the impossible predicament faced by one whose battle with a cruel and degenerative illness is now over, and another man whose battle with Alzheimer's continues.[7]*

Yes, it is absolutely right that we should respond with empathy and compassion to those who experience extremely distressing conditions. But I suspect that many do not have to be exhorted to engage

---

7   *Radio Times*, 11-17 June 2011

empathetically in such situations. It is often instinctive for us to do so, and, at the same time, to picture ourselves in similar circumstances. That can leave us imagining that we couldn't cope and that we would wish to die—and would want to be helped to do so. Again, fear of the future for ourselves is often what drives the debate, and has led to the growing support for assisted suicide among the general public. But these issues are so serious that it is important that we do not simply respond to them in that way. We cannot afford "to leave the debate behind". We need, rather, to be encouraged to engage not just empathetically, but also with a sober consideration of crucial moral, theological and practical concerns. An emotional response based on fear of loss of dignity must not be the determinative factor.

It is important to stress that the fear of what might happen is often much worse than the reality, especially when the best standards of palliative care are applied. For example, information from St Christopher's Hospice in London, where modern palliative care began, has show that 94% of over 200 MND patients died peacefully and, contrary to some media hype, none of them choked to death.[8]

Incidentally, Sir Terry, who believed in the right

---

8   Dr. Peter Saunders, "Assisted dying" editorial, *Triple Helix*, spring 2006 issue, p3

to choose an assisted death, died naturally of a chest infection in 2015, surrounded by his family and with his cat on his bed.[9]

5. COST

The previous arguments are often personal, but there is another, external reason why support for assisted suicide is growing. Living longer is a costly business, especially if you are disabled or have lost your mental capacity.

As the growing demographic problem of old age became clearer to see, British author Martin Amis expressed the concern eloquently when he posed the question, "How is the country going to survive this silver tsunami?"

By 2033, 23 per cent of the UK population will be 65 or over. If the population hits 70 million by 2029, as recently forecast by the Office for National Statistics (ONS), that will mean the working population will have to support at least 16 million people of current retirement age by 2033. The fastest increase is in the "oldest old", who need much more care and support than younger pensioners.

In the light of these realities, moral philosopher Mary Warnock has commented:

---

9   "Sir Terry Pratchett, renowned fantasy author, dies aged 66." *BBC News.* 12/3/15.

> *If you're demented, you're wasting people's lives—your family's lives and you're wasting the resources of the National Health Service… if somebody absolutely, desperately, wants to die because they're a burden to their family, or the state, then I think they too should be allowed to die.*[10]

Amis suggested, perhaps tongue in cheek, the building of euthanasia booths on street corners, where old people "could get a Martini and a medal" before taking their life.[11]

Put together, these are powerful arguments for assisted suicide—especially when they are wrapped up in emotional stories, like those in chapter 1. Resistance to a change in the law in the UK and many parts of the US remains strong, but public opinion in both countries has moved increasingly in favour of legalising assisted suicide. Recent assisted dying bills in the UK Parliament were voted down, but 71% of the public supported them.

Against this landscape of increasing acceptance and demands for a change in the law, what stance should a Christian take? What are the arguments against a right to die?

---

10 *Daily Telegraph*, 19/9/08

11 *Sunday Times*, 24/1/10

THE CASE AGAINST

CHAPTER FOUR

Before considering a number of practical arguments against assisted suicide, I want to focus on the huge issues that stand behind the debate. Most of these centre on our view of humanity itself.

1. THE VALUE AND MEANING OF HUMAN LIFE

Much of the drive for assisted suicide is promoted by a secular view, that we are nothing but naked apes. To quote Gilbert and Sullivan:

> *"Darwinian man, though well-behaved,*
> *At best is only a monkey shaved* [12]

---

12 W. S. Gilbert. Lady Psyche in *Princess Ida*, act 2. cited in: Andrews, Robert, *The Columbia Dictionary of Quotations*, (Columbia University Press, 1993), p294

Many people now believe the view that we are just highly evolved animals; we and everything else in the world have emerged purely by chance, as a result of impersonal scientific processes. The rejection of a creator leads to radical independence.

But contrary to the prevailing opinion, the Bible teaches that we are not autonomous individuals. Christians differ on how the creation accounts in Genesis 1–2 are to be read and the extent to which God used scientific processes, but all agree that we have been created by him. We are not free to choose whatever we want to. We are created beings who have been **designed** by a loving creator.

> *Then God said, "Let us make mankind in our image, in our likeness, so that they may rule over the fish in the sea and the birds in the sky, over the livestock and all the wild animals, and over all the creatures that move along the ground."*
>
> *So God created mankind in his own image,*
> *in the image of God he created them;*
> *male and female he created them.*
>
> Genesis 1 v 26-27

God gives human beings great responsibility as the rulers of creation under him, but limits are placed upon our freedom. We must never forget our place as creatures in God's world. So, for example, it is not for us to decide when we will end our lives. We should certainly be willing to die if faithfulness to Christ demands it, but accepting the possible consequences of godly obedience is very different from deliberately choosing to die. Martyrdom is honoured by Christians as a noble sacrifice, but suicide is always resisted.

The Bible reveals that because we are *designed* by God, we are also intrinsically **dignified**. Our lives have value and meaning, even when we or other people do not believe that. This is enormously important to understand. Because we are made in the image of God, we cannot treat any human life, including our own, as lacking value and purpose.

We may lose our job, and feel worthless. We are not, because our value does not depend on what we do; it depends on who God has made us. We may fail an exam, or not find a marriage partner, or suffer from a debilitating illness—and think we are worthless. We are not, because our value does not depend on our intelligence, or ability, or marital status, or physical ability; it depends on God, who made us and loves us.

This should also make us see others differently. The most helpless infant, the most vulnerable and incapable disabled person, the most dependent old person who has lost their memory and their ability to cope—all of them have lives that are truly valuable because they are made in the image of God.

The radical independence of the secular worldview leads to fragile dignity. If human beings are just animals, the only thing that distinguishes us from any other form of life is our greater capacities. There is no logical reason to regard a human with limited capacity as having greater dignity or worth than a highly functioning animal. Peter Singer, Professor of Bioethics at Princeton University, has argued that…

> … *once the religious mumbo jumbo surrounding the word "human" has been taken away, we will not regard as sacrosanct the life of every member of our species, no matter how limited its capacity for intelligent or even conscious life may be.*[13]

Singer defines a person as a "self-conscious or rational being who is therefore able to make decisions". It follows then, according to his definition, that some primates are persons and some humans are not, either because they are not fully developed, like a baby in the womb, or because they have impaired capacity, whether from a congenital condition or the

---

13 P. Singer, "Sanctity of Life or Quality of Life?" in *Paediatrics*, 1983, 72:1, p128-9

effects of illness or ageing. It is no surprise that he supports abortion, euthanasia and even, in certain circumstances, infanticide.

I am certainly not suggesting that everyone who rejects the belief that human beings are made in the image of God shares these views. But it is important to recognise that the rejection of an external grounding for universal human dignity robs it of any firm basis. Any criteria that are *internal* to the world, can always be exhibited to a greater or lesser extent. For example, individuals can be more or less rational or responsive. That means that, if determined on those grounds, human dignity will either a) not be equal or b) in being equal, it will set a threshold which can exclude some humans. Only an external grounding for human dignity, which flows from our creation in God's image, and not from any ability or capacity we have, will be both equal and inclusive.

Humanity has an appalling record of "re-categorising" people: African slaves, Australian aboriginals, European Jews, babies in the womb. If we can shift categories and decide that those defined by them are no longer humans, it makes it OK to treat them terribly or even dispose of them. The Bible will not allow us to do that, because we are all made in the image of God—we have built-in value.

Human dignity depends not on what we do but

who we are by creation. God has set us apart from the rest of the created order. That is true of every human being: young and old, born and unborn, able-bodied and disabled, highly intelligent and those with limited cognitive capacity.

Author G. K. Chesterton said:

> *People are equal in the same way pennies are equal. Some are bright, others are dull; some are worn smooth, others are sharp and fresh. But all are equal in value for each penny bears the image of the sovereign; each person bears the image of the King of kings.*[14]

We are *designed* by God and *dignified* by God, and we are also **dependent** upon God. As Paul says to the Athenian philosophers:

> *"He himself gives everyone life and breath and everything else ... For in him we live and move and have our being."* Acts 17 v 25, 28

In Job's words, repeated at many funerals:

> *The Lord gave and the Lord has taken away; may the name of the Lord be praised."*
>
> Job 1 v 21

---

14 Atributed to G. K. Chesterton and cited in Tim Chester, *Good News to the Poor* (Leicester: IVP, 2004), p24

God has the power over life and death. We are forbidden from taking our own lives and from murdering others.

2. THE DIGNITY OF INTERDEPENDENCE

There is another important aspect to our created-ness that bears strongly on this debate, and is often forgotten or ignored. We are not only *dependent on God*, but we are also made to be **dependent on each other**—we are built for community. In the Bible God is revealed as Trinity. The three Persons of the Godhead are mutually dependent, united by their eternal relationships. And human beings, created in the image of this triune God, are designed for relationship with him and with one another. We are bound together in community. That truth is often unrecognised by those who stress individual autonomy when advocating assisted suicide. But the reality is that when an individual takes their own life, their death inevitably has a profound impact on others, above all on their family and friends, but also on the wider community. The thought is expressed powerfully in John Donne's famous poem:

No man is an island entire of itself; every man
is a piece of the continent, a part of the main.
If a clod be washed away by the sea, Europe

is the less, as well as if a promontory were,
as well as if a manor of thy friend's or of thine
own were: any man's death diminishes me,
because I am involved in mankind,
and therefore never send to know for whom
the bell tolls; it tolls for thee.[15]

We are not autonomous individuals. God has designed us to live in relationship. When we are born, we are absolutely and utterly dependent on others. As we grow, and for much of our lives, most of us are able to fend for ourselves, but we still rely on a web of human relationships. At other times, when we are ill or have specific needs, and particularly as we grow old and frail, we will depend more on others again, perhaps to the extent we did as infants.

My father found the loss of independence the hardest aspect of his illness to cope with. It was hugely frustrating for him to have to rely increasingly on others, although he gradually accepted this. At the very end of his life he was paralysed and unable to speak. Those last few days were intensely sad and yet also, in a strange way, pro-

---

15 Meditation XVII, *Devotions upon Emergent Occasions* by John Donne

foundly beautiful. He had given so much to us and now we in the family had the privilege of caring for him, stroking and kissing him, singing his favourite hymns and praying. Such dependence is not undignified. This is being human.

3. SUFFERING IS NOT THE ULTIMATE EVIL

This third argument is perhaps the most difficult for those who are not Christians to understand and embrace, but it comes from the very heart of our faith. Having rejected God, life for many people is, at some level or other, about the maximisation of pleasure, and the minimisation of pain.

Suffering is therefore seen as being entirely negative and to be avoided at all costs. As a result, if we hold this view, we will do all we can to anaesthetise our pain, whether physical or emotional, not just with medication, but through retail therapy or alcohol, or perhaps recreational drugs and pornography—anything to take it away. And we will long for a pain-free death, ideally in our sleep but, otherwise, why not with medical assistance?

Joni Eareckson Tada, who was left permanently paralysed after a diving accident and has been a wonderful Christian example in the face of suffering, has summed up the attitude of many:

If our culture can't fix it, cure it, medicate it, sedate it or surgically remove it, then please get rid of it—because we sure can't live with it.[16]

Our therapeutic society has already taken frightening strides towards the vision of the "Brave New World" that Aldous Huxley describes in his novel. He imagines a world in which biotechnology has been used to create an environment in which pain and suffering have been almost entirely eradicated, and where what little remains is soon dealt with by the instant feel-good drug "soma". Superficially, we might think that this is heaven on earth, but it is in fact a kind of hell—a saccharine world starved of everything that makes life worth living. One character, disgusted by the control exercised over people by the World State, cries out:

But I don't want comfort. I want God, I want poetry, I want real danger, I want freedom, I want goodness, I want sin ... I'm claiming the right to be unhappy.[17]

Huxley realised that it is not enough for human

---

16 Joni Eareckson Tada and Nigel Cameron, *How to be a Christian in a Brave New World*, (Grand Rapids: Zondervan, 2006), p137

17 Aldous Huxley, *Brave New World*, (London: Vintage Books), p211-212

beings just to be comfortable and pain-free. Deep down we yearn for more than that.

The Bible never suggests that suffering is good in and of itself. Far from it! Like death, it is a result of the fall and God's judgment on human sin. But it is certainly not outside of God's loving, sovereign control of all things. In fact, he is able to use it in ways that help us see what life is all about.

There is certainly mystery here, but I have often seen this reality, both in my own life and in the lives of others. Although we may not notice it at the time, many of us can testify, as we look back, that it has been through the hardest times that we have grown most in our dependence on and joyful trust in God. This is an illustration of the biblical principle that God can use the fire of suffering to refine us and produce the gold of strengthened faith (1 Peter 1 v 7).

The ultimate proof that suffering is not meaningless for Christian believers is the suffering and death of the Lord Jesus Christ. It was through the cross that forgiveness, new life and a restored relationship with God were made possible. And it is through his death that we are brought together as God's new community—the church—united to each other for ever. That is why the symbol of our faith is a cross. It is why we regularly remember his suffering and death with the symbols of bread and wine. He shows us that suffering can be purposeful.

That means it is even possible to have a good death. God can powerfully use the experience of dying in our own lives and the lives of others. Many people today will say, "When I die, I'd like to go suddenly in my sleep". That's an expression of the fear of suffering that we were thinking about earlier. But this is a modern obsession. In earlier times it used to be felt that those who died suddenly had missed out.

A warning of impending death provides the opportunity to focus on what really matters. It can give time and space to put relationships right and express love, forgiveness and gratitude. Dying can also be a profound spiritual help. I have seen a number of people engage seriously with the gospel for the first time after facing a terminal diagnosis and, as a result, come to faith in Christ. Many others, who have been Christians already, have grown deeply in their spiritual life. One young man stands out in my mind. He had been a fairly half-hearted believer but, through the experience of facing cancer, he grew immeasurably in maturity as a man and as a Christian. Even as his body was dying, his spirit became visibly more and more alive.

These are the big principles from Scripture that Christians will want to focus on in any conversation about death and dying. We believe that we are made in God's image and are therefore intrinsically valuable. So we do not have the right to end our own lives, or the lives of others. We believe that God has made us to be intimately bound to each other in community, and that our actions affect and influence others. And we believe that suffering is not the ultimate evil, but can, in God's purposes, have value. We can die a good death.

PRACTICAL ARGUMENTS

On top of these specifically Christian perspectives on assisted suicide, there are a number of practical arguments that should also concern us. Here they are in brief:

1. The elderly and chronically infirm may feel pressured. If assisted suicide becomes a legal and cheap "treatment" option, it is very easy to imagine how vulnerable people could feel it was their duty to die, so as not to be a burden on others. It is for this reason that all the major disability-rights organisations in Britain oppose a change in the law. As we have already seen, in Washington State, USA, 61% of those ending their life cited a concern that they might be a burden if they lived as one of the reasons for their choice.[18]

---

18 See page 27.

2. It cheapens life. People who wish to end their lives are declaring "my life is not worth living". As soon as society allows them to take the next step and receive help to die, we are effectively saying, "We agree with you" or, at the very least, we could be heard to be saying that. As a result, those facing similar circumstances could easily feel less valued. This is one of the ways in which, in the words of ethicist Nigel Biggar, "the legalisation of intentional medical killing threatens to give us a radically liberal society at the expense of a substantially humane one".[19]

3. The grounds for assisted suicide are likely to be extended. Attempts to introduce a change in the law tend to begin with limited proposals; for example, making provision for the terminally ill. But experience elsewhere suggests that this would just be a first step towards progressive liberalisation. There is certainly no logical reason why that should not occur. If the argument used for assisted suicide was autonomy, why should that be limited to those facing imminent death? Or if the basis was a desire to relieve people of suffering, why should

---

19 Nigel Biggar, "A Case Against Permitting Intentional Medical Killing", in *Ethics in Brief*, Kirby Laing Institute, Autumn 2009, Vol. 14 No. 1

that not also apply to those facing psychological distress or who are simply tired or life? This is actually beginning to happen in the Netherlands. The *Guardian* newspaper recently reported that, "The Dutch government intends to draft a law that would legalise assisted suicide for people who feel they have 'completed life', but are not necessarily terminally ill."[20] This is barely 15 years since assisted suicide was legalised in 2002.

4. It is possible to decide to kill yourself based on the wrong diagnosis. There are some recorded instances of this, as well as people who have decided to end their lives only for some remarkable treatment to be made available soon after their deaths, which they could have made use of had they not gone ahead with their assisted suicide. Even when the diagnosis is right, the prognosis may well not be. Many patients live for longer than the period of time they have been told.[21]

5. The impact on doctors, and their patients' relationships with them. The introduction of assisted

---

20 https://www.theguardian.com/world/2016/oct/13/netherlands-may-allow-assisted-dying-for-those-who-feel-life-is-complete

21 http://euthanasiadebate.org.nz/mistaken-diagnosis-of-terminal-illness-is-not-uncommon/

suicide would result in an inevitable strain on doctors, many of whom would no longer only have responsibility for promoting their patients' health but also, sometimes, for helping kill them. That would surely lead to an erosion of trust between patients and doctors.

Euthanasia is gaining ground as an option in our culture, and law-makers are being repeatedly pressed to change the law. By renaming it with cosier titles such as "assisted dying" or "easeful dying", the campaign groups have made it seem and feel more attractive. Fear of dementia, disability and death has played on our imaginations, and support for assisted dying is at an all-time high. But it is vital that the law remains clear. A departure from the principle that "killing people is wrong" will put us on a slippery slope that will have serious consequences for us all.

FACING DEATH

CHAPTER FIVE

When the old man Simeon met Christ as an infant in the temple, he broke out into a song of praise:

> *Sovereign Lord, as you have promised,*
>   *you may now dismiss your servant in peace.*
> *For my eyes have seen your salvation,*
>   *which you have prepared in the sight of all*
> *nations:*
> *a light for revelation to the Gentiles,*
>   *and the glory of your people Israel.*
>
> Luke 2 v 29-32

More than anyone else, Christians should be able to think and speak about death and dying with hope, confidence, meaning and purpose. More than that, we are in a position to speak directly to the fears people have about their future. Here are some thoughts about how we can make a positive contribution, not just to the political and ethical debate, but also in our conversations with others about the end of life.

1. IF YOU HAVE SUICIDAL THOUGHTS

First, I want to speak directly to anyone who is reading this book who may be feeling very low, perhaps because you are depressed, ill or disabled. When we are at our lowest, suicidal thoughts are very common, and can become a pattern. Christians are not immune from this. The thought of ending your own life can be a relief when you are weighed down with loneliness, worries or pain. But too easily these feelings can move from vague thoughts, to a plan, to a dummy run, and then even an attempt.

My dearest brother, sister, *please resist these suicidal thoughts*. It's not your life to take; you belong to God. And you are bonded to others—to family, friends, your fellowship—in ways that run much deeper than you may recognise at the moment.

I want to say to you, not glibly, *please trust God.* He loves you; his Son died for you. Things may seem very dark for you, but if you trust him, his Holy Spirit will help you. You are walking through "the valley of the shadow of death" but the Lord, your Shepherd, is with you, even if you cannot see it or feel it.

And please seek help wherever you can find it: from your doctor, your pastor, your church fellowship. When we bring our dark thoughts out into the open, we often gain a better perspective on them. Don't let fear that people will think you odd or strange hold you back from talking to others, and to your heavenly Father. It may also help to read an encouraging passage from the Bible (e.g. Psalm 23 or Psalm 46). Ask God to help you trust that his word and his promises to you are true—even if you find it hard to believe at this moment.

2. CARING FOR OTHERS

Care for the needy and for families has always been at the heart of the Christian call for compassion and mercy for the helpless.

From the earliest times, the church provided for widows and orphans (see Acts 6 v 1-6). This instinct is a practical outworking of the gospel. In Christ, God cared for us when we were weak, helpless and defenceless. So it follows that Christ's disciples should show the same compassion for others. As years went by, care and medicine for the poor were woven into the structure of the Christian church. Wherever the gospel message has gone around the world, the benefits of medicine, health and social compassion have followed.

But this care is not just the preserve of the church as a whole. Practical love and mercy are expected of individual believers as well. In a passage giving instructions on care for elderly widows, Paul gives Timothy a strong warning to pass on to the believers he serves:

> *Anyone who does not provide for their relatives, and especially for their own household, has denied the faith and is worse than an unbeliever.*   1 Timothy 5 v 8

So whatever the provision of care from the state, or from the church, the first line of responsibility that Christians will want to embrace is the care we show to our family members, and by extension, the care we show to brothers and sisters in our Christian family.

We should resist the temptation to choose the option which causes us least trouble, but rather, ask what would be best for the individual. Our society is too quick to put people into residential care, although many sick, disabled or elderly people would be happier and thrive more in our families.

The time may come when full-time professional help is needed, but we will still need to ensure we visit regularly and maintain close contact. This may still be very costly in time, money and emotional energy. One friend of mine is encouraged to persevere in her care for her mother, who has dementia, by repeating the words of 1 Timothy 5 v 4 to herself: "This is pleasing to God".

Others can still live independently and may be able to cope with their practical needs, but still require special attention. Ageing and illness are often accompanied by emotional or social isolation. In the UK 1 in 6 of the elderly feel socially isolated and that figure increases to 72% among those who are over 85. It is our responsibility to ensure that our family members do not feel cut off in that way. Churches will also need to help. We are not judged by numbers or activity, but rather, by the depth and breadth of love we have. If we are able to look after the lonely, elderly and disabled, we are showing they have value, dignity and meaning. Such love and compassion is part of our gospel calling as Christians.

3. ENGAGING WITH OUR CULTURE

We are all citizens, and therefore our views and perspectives have an important part to play in a national debate. When problems are so complex, the temptation is to withdraw into my own quiet life and the comfort of my own church; but it is really important that we are engaged in society. That engagement must include action, not just words.

In the ancient world, infanticide and assisted suicide were very common practices; but, because of their convictions about the value and dignity of human life made in the image of God, Christians modelled a very different approach. They cared for the sick, they adopted and gave homes to abandoned children, and they looked after the sick and dying. We today must follow their example. Our involvement in this issue must not just mean campaigning. Why should we expect people to listen to us if we are not prepared to back up our words with costly action? Through our loving, sacrificial care for the needy and vulnerable in our families, churches and wider community, we must ensure that it is obvious how much we value every individual life.

But we must also make our voice heard on this question in the public square. So much of the pressure for change is based on emotional responses to heartrending cases and personal fears about the future. Advances in palliative care, significantly pioneered by Christians like Dame Cicely Saunders, now mean that many of these fears are unfounded. Best practice is concerned to alleviate, not just physical pain, but also the emotional, spiritual and relational pain of the dying, and can make an enormous difference. Christians should be promoting a greater awareness of what is available, and arguing for adequate funding to ensure that everyone can receive it.

It is also important that people are helped to recognise the likely consequences of assisted suicide (see the practical arguments of pages 49-52). These do not depend on biblical foundations and may be as far as it is possible to go in some situations. But, when appropriate, Christians will also want to speak about the convictions that undergird our position. We must never be heard only to be saying "no". Our message is a gloriously positive one: the great value of every human life, the dignity of mutual dependence, and the sovereign love of God working in and through suffering, as seen supremely in Christ.

4. BE REALISTIC ABOUT THE END OF LIFE

This series is called *Talking Points* and deals with issues that Christians need to reach a more settled mind about. The first step is therefore to talk with one another about death, dying and assisted suicide. We are not immune from our culture's aversion to talking about these things, but we have a valuable and positive perspective to encourage each other with, and to speak to others about.

But please don't think that end-of-life decisions will always be straightforward. Christians believe in life, because we believe in the God who is the author and giver of life. But we also believe in death as a reality in our fallen world. It is not always right to pour huge amounts of money and effort into keeping someone alive; sometimes it is best to let them die. Encouraging them to cling on and receive every possible treatment is not always advisable.

Best practice among medics recognises the distinction between *intention* and *foresight*. This is known as "the principle of double effect". Doctors, with the support of close relatives, may decide that it is in the best interests of a patient to withdraw intensive life support or to give a high dosage of painkilling drugs. They may foresee that this action is likely to shorten life, but that is not the *intention*. The patient may die, for example, from the higher dose of morphine that is needed to relieve the pain. But the aim is not to kill but to *relieve suffering*. This is entirely appropriate and moral.

5. BELIEVE THE GOOD NEWS ABOUT LIFE BEYOND DEATH

We believe in a risen Saviour, and that death is not the end, but the doorway to eternity. We need to be ready to face death in a Christian way. Not fearfully, grasping at any hope for a reprieve, but confident in our own salvation. We must be prepared to say with

Simeon: "Sovereign Lord, as you have promised, you may now dismiss your servant in peace". We must be willing to submit to the sovereign hand of God, who gave us life, and who, in his own time and his own way, will withdraw it again.

Last year, a friend of mine died aged 48. But his brother, who spoke at the funeral, told us that he had been ready for death for 34 years, since he first put his trust in Christ as a teenager. As a result, he approached death full of confidence. Are you ready?

6. SHARE THE GOOD NEWS OF LIFE BEYOND DEATH

Engaging with people who are dying will present an opportunity to share the Christian hope. We do not subscribe to the bleak worldview of a world without God—that when we are dead, we are gone. Nor do we cover over the reality of death with sentimentality. Death is real, because sin is real. And there is a judgment to face after death. But there is also real hope. Hope, because the suffering and death of the Lord Jesus Christ can bring us safely through the judgment. Hope, because Jesus rose from the grave on the third day and has defeated death. Hope, because he promises an eternity of joy-filled life to those who place their trust in him. The process of dying may still be bitter, and the heartache of those

who suffer grief is real—but death has lost its sting.
So Christians can face the grave with the certain
hope of what is to come when Christ returns:

> *He will wipe every tear from their eyes.*
> *There will be no more death or mourning*
> *or crying or pain, for the old order of things*
> *has passed away.*   Revelation 21 v 4

FURTHER READING

Right to Die? Euthanasia, Assisted suicide and End-of-life Care, John Wyatt (IVP, Nottingham, 2015)

Matters of Life and Death, John Wyatt (IVP, Nottingham, 2009)

Assisted Suicide: CMF Files No. 56, Rick Thomas (Christian Medical Fellowship, London, 2015). Download from www.cmf.org.uk

"A Case Against Permitting Intentional Medical Killing", Nigel Biggar, in *Ethics in Brief,* (Kirby Laing Institute, Autumn 2009), Vol. 14 No. 1

I Just Want to Die: Replacing Suicidal Thoughts with Hope, David Powlison (New Growth Press, 2010)

Making the Most of the Rest of your Life, John Chapman (Matthias Media, Sydney, 2011).

Could it Be Dementia? Louise Morse (Monarch, Oxford, 2008)

Dementia: Pathways to Hope. Spiritual Insights and Practical Advice for Carers, Louise Morse (Lion, Oxford 2015)

Dementia: Living in the Memories of God, John Swinton (Eerdemans, Grand Rapids, 2012).

Second Forgetting: remembering the power of the Gospel during Alzheimer's Disease, Dr Benjamin Mast (Zondervan, Grand Rapids, 2014).

On death, dying and grief
A Grief Observed, C. S. Lewis (Faber & Faber, 2013)

Hearing Jesus Speak into Your Sorrow, Nancy Guthrie (Tyndale, 2009)

Surprised by Suffering: The Role of Pain and Death in the Christian Life, R. C. Sproul (Reformation Trust Publishing, 2010)

Walking with God through Pain and Suffering, Tim Keller (Riverhead Books, 2014)

Why Suffering? Finding Meaning and Comfort When Life Doesn't Make Sense, Ravi Zacharias and Vince Vitale (FaithWords, 2014)

On My Way to Heaven, Mark Ashton (10publishing, 2010)

ACKNOWLEDGEMENTS

Once again Tim Thornborough as editor and my colleague Luke Cornelius have greatly contributed to this book. Konyew Kwek's and Stuart Ramsay's comments on the manuscript have been very helpful.

My whole family want to express our gratitude to all those at Southampton General and Basingstoke and North Hampshire Hospitals who gave superb medical care to my father when he was ill, and especially to the team in Ward E4 in Basingstoke, who cared for him in his final days.

ASSISTED SUICIDE
DISCUSSION GUIDE

This series does not aim to say everything there is to say about a subject, but to give an overview and a solid grounding to how Christians should start to think about the issue from the Bible. We hope that as you discuss this book, and the Bible passages that it is based on, you will gain in confidence to speak faithfully, compassionately and wisely to others.

Below is an extensive list of questions. Please pick and choose the ones that suit your group, and the time you have available. If you are leading a group, try to keep constantly in people's minds that this is not simply a discussion about a political or moral "issue"—but that these are about choices being made by real people who are, perhaps, suffering deeply, and need our love compassion, and above all the gospel message of hope.

TO START
- **Share your stories:** What are your experiences of people who have had an illness, or are of advancing years, and have thought about how they might "end it all"?
- What stage are you at in your own life? Do you have elderly parents or relatives who you have the responsibility to care for? Or do you have other dependants who may think that taking their lives is a positive option?
- Before you started reading this book, what were your thoughts about what the Christian view of assisted suicide was or should be?

- Look at the quotes on page 12. How do you react to each of them? Do you find yourself agreeing or disagreeing with any of them?

CHAPTER 1: A COMPLEX PROBLEM

- How do you react to the three stories that the chapter begins with? Do you empathise with the situations these people found themselves in?
- Look at the definitions on pages 18-19. Are there any you don't understand—or are there words and ideas that you have heard used differently?

CHAPTER 2: A GROWING PROBLEM

- **Thinking about death**. In your experience are people open to talking about death, or embarrassed by the mere mention of it? How do you feel about discussing your own death?
- Have you ever seen a dead person, or been with someone when they died? What were your thoughts and feelings?
- *How would you like to die?* If you asked people that question, what might they answer? How would you answer it?
- If there was a national vote to allow assisted suicide, how do you think most people would vote? How would you vote?

CHAPTER 3: THE RIGHT TO DIE

- What do you think of the arguments in favour: pain; freedom; quality of life; dependence and dignity; and cost?

- Which of these do you think is the strongest in purely rational human terms?
- Which of these arguments do you react most strongly against as a Christian? Can you justify your reaction from the Bible?

CHAPTER 4: THE CASE AGAINST

- **We are designed, and therefore dignified, and also dependent on God.** How is this Christian view completely at odds with the views of others? Is this how you see yourself?
- How does this view change the way we see everyone—including those who are disabled, incapable, or infirm?
- **We are dependent on each other.** How is this Christian view completely at odds with the views of others? Is this how you see yourself in your relationships with others?
- How does this change the way we think about assisted suicide and other end-of-life questions?
- **Suffering is not the ultimate evil.** Is this idea new to you? How would others you know who are not Christian react to this suggestion? How would you argue positively for this view with them?
- What experiences have you had that confirm this truth?
- Which of the practical arguments at the end of the chapter are you most moved by? In conversation with others do you think we should use these practical arguments first, or only after expressing the Christian position with the other arguments in the chapter?

CHAPTER 5: FACING DEATH

- "More than anyone else, Christians should be able to think and speak about death and dying with hope, confidence, meaning and purpose" (p53). Is that true for you? If you got into a conversation with someone who was dying, or caring for someone who was dying, what are your fears about how well or badly you would handle the conversation?

- **Suicidal thoughts:** Have you ever contemplated suicide—perhaps just imagining it? What did you do with those thoughts? How would you help/advise/talk with someone who was a Christian who has such thoughts?

- **Caring for others:** Who in your church is caring sacrificially for a dependant? What particular needs do carers have? How might the fellowship be better involved in supporting them?

- **Engaging with our culture:** Do you know the current state of play in the law, and any proposed changes where you live? How might you get involved in the debate or support those who are representing a Christian voice in the discussion? As we get involved, how can we honour Christ in the way we conduct ourselves, as well as the truths we put forward?

- **Be realistic about death and dying.** Are you? Do you talk about these things with others—with your children and parents? Or is the subject of death and dying off the table for some reason? How can you start to talk about it?

- **Believe the good news about life beyond death.** Do you? We can all be plagued by doubts. How can we address those doubts in ourselves, and with each other?

- **Share the good news of life beyond death.** How do you feel about sharing the good news of Jesus with someone who is dying—a relative or a friend? Share any experiences you have had in doing this. How can we do that sensitively, but with the right kind of urgency?

TO FINISH

- What's the big thing that has impacted you from reading *Assisted Suicide*?
- How will you think about and pray for those who are contemplating assisted suicide?
- What extra help and information do you think you need to be more confident about what you believe on this subject?

PRAY

- Ask God to help you understand the issue and the people better.
- Pray that your church fellowship would be supportive of those caring for the elderly and infirm.
- Pray for any people you may know who are approaching death, and for their families and friends who are seeking to give Christian care and counsel to them.

Printable copies of this discussion guide are available at:
www.thegoodbook.co.uk/talking-points-assisted-suicide
www.thegoodbook.com/talking-points-assisted-suicide

A TALKING POINTS BOOK BY
VAUGHAN ROBERTS

TRANSGENDER

There's been huge cultural change in the last few decades. Same-sex marriage would have been unthinkable 20 or 30 years ago. Now it's almost universally accepted in the Western world. Suddenly the issue of transgender is the next big social, cultural issue that is dominating the headlines.

Vaughan Roberts surveys the Christian worldview and seeks to apply the principles he uncovers to the many complex questions surrounding gender identity. This short book gives an overview and a starting point for constructive discussion as we seek to live in a world with different values, and to love, serve and relate to transgender people.

Talking Points is a series of short books designed to help Christians think and talk about today's big issues, and to relate to others with compassion, conviction and wisdom.

> *"In this brief book on a complex subject Vaughan Roberts combines the traditional Christian understanding of gender and the body with a very careful, loving, understanding stance toward transgender people. The two almost never go together, and that's why this book is so good!"*

Tim Keller, pastor, author and Vice-President of
The Gospel Coalition

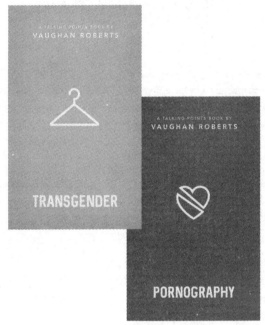

thegoodbook

COMPANY

Opening up the Bible

At The Good Book Company, we are dedicated to helping Christians and local churches grow. We believe that God's growth process always starts with hearing clearly what he has said to us through his timeless word—the Bible.

Ever since we opened our doors in 1991, we have been striving to produce resources that honour God in the way the Bible is used. We have grown to become an international provider of user-friendly resources to the Christian community, with believers of all backgrounds and denominations using our Bible studies, books, evangelistic resources, DVD-based courses and training events.

We want to equip ordinary Christians to live for Christ day by day, and churches to grow in their knowledge of God, their love for one another, and the effectiveness of their outreach.

Call us for a discussion of your needs or visit one of our local websites for more information on the resources and services we provide.

Your friends at The Good Book Company

NORTH AMERICA
UK & EUROPE
AUSTRALIA
NEW ZEALAND

 thegoodbook.com
thegoodbook.co.uk
thegoodbook.com.au
thegoodbook.co.nz

 866 244 2165
0333 123 0880
(02) 9564 3555
(+64) 3 343 2463

 WWW.CHRISTIANITYEXPLORED.ORG
Our partner site is a great place for those exploring the Christian faith, with a clear explanation of the good news, powerful testimonies and answers to difficult questions.